BUILDING AN AIRPORT

BY KAREN LATCHANA KENNEY

SEQUENCE

AMICUS | AMICUS INK

Sequence is published by Amicus and Amicus Ink
P.O. Box 1329, Mankato, MN 56002
www.amicuspublishing.us

Library of Congress Cataloging-in-Publication Data
Names: Kenney, Karen Latchana, author.
Title: Building an airport / by Karen Latchana Kenney.
Description: Mankato, MN : Amicus and Amicus Ink, [2020] | Series: Sequence.Amazing structures | Includes index. | Audience: Grades 4 to 6.
Identifiers: LCCN 2019006256 (print) | LCCN 2019007369 (ebook) | ISBN 9781681518718 (pdf) | ISBN 9781681518312 (library binding) | ISBN 9781681525594 (pbk.)
Subjects: LCSH: Airports--Juvenile literature.
Classification: LCC TL725.15 (ebook) | LCC TL725.15 .K46 2020 (print) | DDC 690/.539--dc23
LC record available at https://lccn.loc.gov/2019006256

Editor: Wendy Dieker
Designer: Ciara Beitlich
Photo Researcher: Shane Freed

Photo Credits: iStock/EvrenKalinbacak cover; Shutterstock/phive cover; Shutterstock/Lukas Gojda 5; iStock/RichLegg 6; iStock/BartCo 8–9; Shutterstock/Iurii Osadchi 10–11; Getty/Simon McGill 13; Getty/ewg3D 14–15; WikiMedia Commons/Joel Martinez 17; Alamy/Spectral 18; Shutterstock/Bartlomiej K. Kwieciszewski 20–21; Shutterstock/Pavel L Photo and Video 22; U.S. Air Force/Airman 1st Class Alan Ricker 25; Shutterstock/AlenKadr 26–27; Getty/Jenner Images 29

Printed in the United States of America

HC 10 9 8 7 6 5 4 3 2 1
PB 10 9 8 7 6 5 4 3 2 1

TABLE OF CONTENTS

We Need an Airport

Flying in airplanes is the fastest way to travel far distances. Airports are the places people go to when they want to fly. Every state has at least one airport. But as a city grows, the people need a better way to fly. What does the city do? It decides to build its own airport.

LOADING . . . LOADING . . . LOADING . . .

A new airport will let more people take off to faraway places.

OADING . . . LOADING . . . LOADING . . .

A new airport will change the landscape of this city.

The city finds a place to build the airport.

YEAR 1

LOADING . . . LOADING . .

Airport Planning

The first step is to make plans. An airport takes up a lot of space. It creates more traffic. Airplanes make a lot of noise, too. The city hires a company to study the area. The company suggests the best place for the airport. It figures out where new roads could be. But more studies need to be done.

LOADING . . . LOADING . . . LOADING . . .

The next step is to test the **site** where the airport will be. The city hires **engineers**. They check the soil. Airplanes need solid ground to land on. Is the ground too wet? Is it hard enough? They also study the plants and animals in the area. Will building there harm the environment? The engineers pick the best site for this project.

An engineer uses special tools to take samples of the soil in the area.

The city finds a place to build the airport.

YEAR 1

YEAR 2

...DING...LOADING...

Engineers find the best site for the new airport.

LOADING... LOADING... LOADING...

The city finds a place to build the airport.

YEAR 1

YEAR 2

Engineers find the best site for the new airport.

YEAR 4

Architects and engineers design the new airport.

...LOADING...

After the site is chosen, the city hires **architects** and engineers. They design the buildings and runways. They plan out the parking ramps. They draw **blueprints**. These are diagrams that show where walls, doors, and windows will be. They show where pipes and wires need to go. This team makes plans for the entire **airport complex**.

A computer drawing shows how a new airport complex will look.

LOADING... LOADING... LOADING...

Preparing to Build

The planning is done. Now the city hires a **contractor**. This company manages the project from start to finish. It has all the big machinery needed to build an airport. It keeps the project on schedule. The contractor also hires workers to build, pour concrete, place pipes and wires, and do finishing work.

Contractors have huge cranes and other equipment for big building projects.

YEAR 1: The city finds a place to build the airport.

YEAR 2: Engineers find the best site for the new airport.

YEAR 4: Architects and engineers design the new airport.

YEAR 5: The city hires a contractor to build the airport complex.

ADING . . .

LOADING...LOADING...LOADING...

A big dump truck carries dirt out of the building site.

- YEAR 1: The city finds a place to build the airport.
- YEAR 2: Engineers find the best site for the new airport.
- YEAR 4: Architects and engineers design the new airport.
- YEAR 5: The city hires a contractor to build the airport complex.
- YEAR 6: Trees are cut down and the land is cleared.

After five years of planning, the site work can finally begin. Workers start clearing the land. The airport is huge. And airplanes need a large amount of open area to land and take off. Trees need to be cut down. Old buildings are torn down. Diggers move dirt. Bulldozers level the ground.

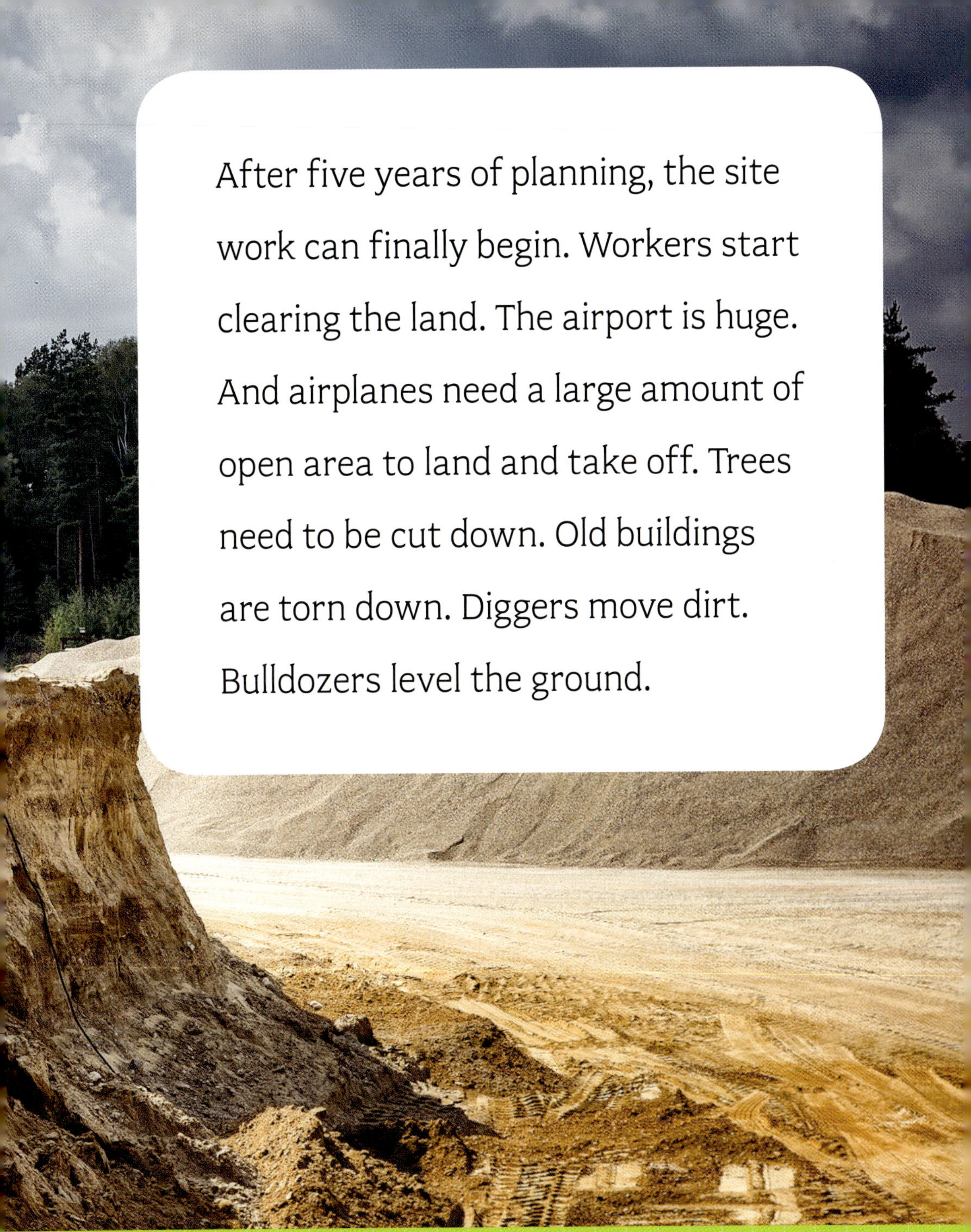

Once the land is cleared, workers prepare the land for a runway. The runway needs to be wide enough and long enough for an airplane to land on. Workers use large machines to flatten the soil. They press down on the soil to remove air pockets. This makes the ground hard and solid. Workers then add a layer of gravel over the soil.

Road rollers pack down gravel to prepare the ground for a runway.

YEAR 1: The city finds a place to build the airport.

YEAR 2: Engineers find the best site for the new airport.

YEAR 4: Architects and engineers design the new airport.

YEAR 5: The city hires a contractor to build the airport complex.

YEAR 6: Trees are cut down and the land is cleared.

Construction workers prepare soil for the runways.

LOADING...LOADING...LOADING...

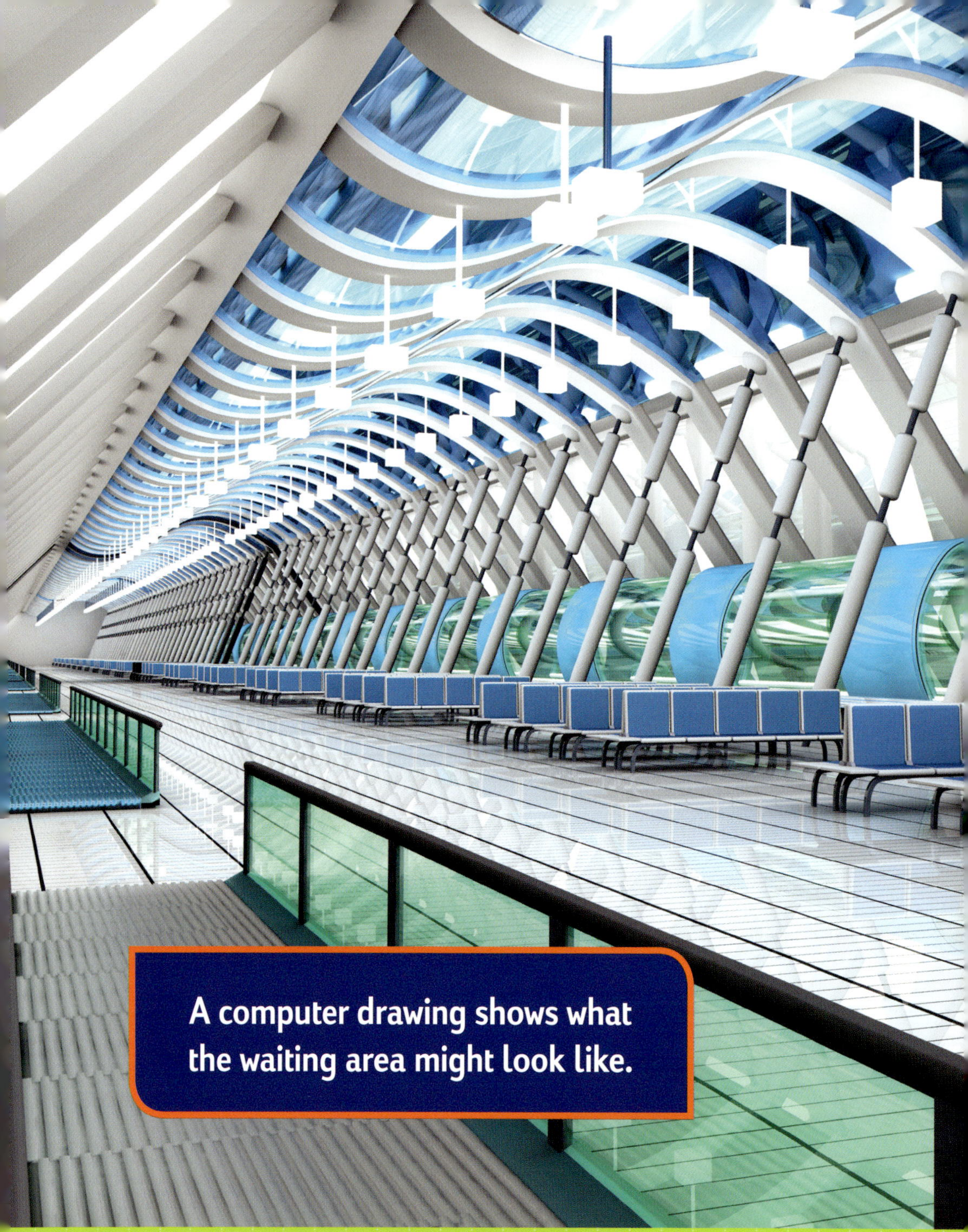

A computer drawing shows what the waiting area might look like.

- The city finds a place to build the airport. (YEAR 1)
- Engineers find the best site for the new airport. (YEAR 2)
- Architects and engineers design the new airport. (YEAR 4)
- The city hires a contractor to build the airport complex. (YEAR 5)
- Trees are cut down and the land is cleared. (YEAR 6)
- Construction workers prepare soil for the runways.

Building the Airport Complex

The airport complex has many buildings. Airplanes are stored in hangars. Parking ramps will hold cars. The **terminal** will have several **concourses**. There will also be ticket counters and baggage claim carousels inside. The airport needs bus and train stations. A hotel will be built for travelers to stay overnight. Architects work on plans for these buildings.

Architects finish plans for buildings.

LOADING . . . LOADING . . .

Workers start on the foundations for all the buildings. They use bulldozers and excavators to move dirt and dig holes. Then they use a **pile** driver to pound long steel rods into the ground. These piles will support the base of the building. On top of the piles, workers pour concrete. This makes the foundations very strong.

A pile driver pounds steel rods into the ground for an airport building.

- YEAR 1 — The city finds a place to build the airport.
- YEAR 2 — Engineers find the best site for the new airport.
- YEAR 4 — Architects and engineers design the new airport.
- YEAR 5 — The city hires a contractor to build the airport complex.
- YEAR 6 — Trees are cut down and the land is cleared.
- Construction workers prepare soil for the runways.

Architects finish plans for buildings.

DING . . . LOADING . . .

Workers build foundations for the buildings.

- **YEAR 1:** The city finds a place to build the airport.
- **YEAR 2:** Engineers find the best site for the new airport.
- **YEAR 4:** Architects and engineers design the new airport.
- **YEAR 5:** The city hires a contractor to build the airport complex.
- **YEAR 6:** Trees are cut down and the land is cleared.
- Construction workers prepare soil for the runways.

Next workers **frame** the buildings. Cranes are used to put up steel beams. Workers add pipes and wires. Walls are put up. Roofs are put on. Windows and doors are installed.

Inside the buildings, workers lay tiles and carpet. Walls are painted. Chairs and counters are installed. Workers add signs and lights.

Workers weld steel beams together for the building frame.

Architects finish plans for buildings.

Workers build foundations for the buildings.

Workers frame and complete the buildings.

YEAR 7

. . . LOADING . . .

One of the most important buildings at the airport is the air traffic control tower. It's tall so controllers can see and direct airplanes. To build it, workers make a tall tube. Then a large crane lifts the control room frame. It places the room on top of the tube. Workers add glass windows all around the control room and finish the inside of the tower.

A crane lifts the control room frame to the top of the air traffic control tower.

YEAR 1: The city finds a place to build the airport.

YEAR 2: Engineers find the best site for the new airport.

YEAR 4: Architects and engineers design the new airport.

YEAR 5: The city hires a contractor to build the airport complex.

YEAR 6: Trees are cut down and the land is cleared.

Construction workers prepare soil for the runways.

Architects finish plans for buildings.

Workers frame and complete the buildings.

YEAR 7

ADING . . .

Workers build foundations for the buildings.

The air traffic control tower is built.

The city finds a place to build the airport.

YEAR 1

Engineers find the best site for the new airport.

YEAR 2

Architects and engineers design the new airport.

YEAR 4

The city hires a contractor to build the airport complex.

YEAR 5

Trees are cut down and the land is cleared.

YEAR 6

Construction workers prepare soil for the runways.

Now it's time to complete the runways. Workers pour concrete into a frame. A large machine slowly moves over it to smooth it out. Another machine cuts grooves in the concrete. This helps water drain off the runway. Then airplanes won't slide when it rains. Workers paint lines and add lights to mark the edges of the runways.

A machine smooths the concrete for the runway.

Architects finish plans for buildings.

Workers build foundations for the buildings.

YEAR 7

Workers frame and complete the buildings.

The air traffic control tower is built.

YEAR 8

Workers pave the runway and add paint and lights.

Ready for Takeoff!

It's taken eight years of planning and building. But now this airport is ready for flights! People crowd inside the terminal. They head down the concourses to their airplanes. Planes take off from the runway. Each day many people visit the airport. Where will they go?

YEAR 1: The city finds a place to build the airport.

YEAR 2: Engineers find the best site for the new airport.

YEAR 4: Architects and engineers design the new airport.

YEAR 5: The city hires a contractor to build the airport complex.

YEAR 6: Trees are cut down and the land is cleared.

Construction workers prepare soil for the runways.

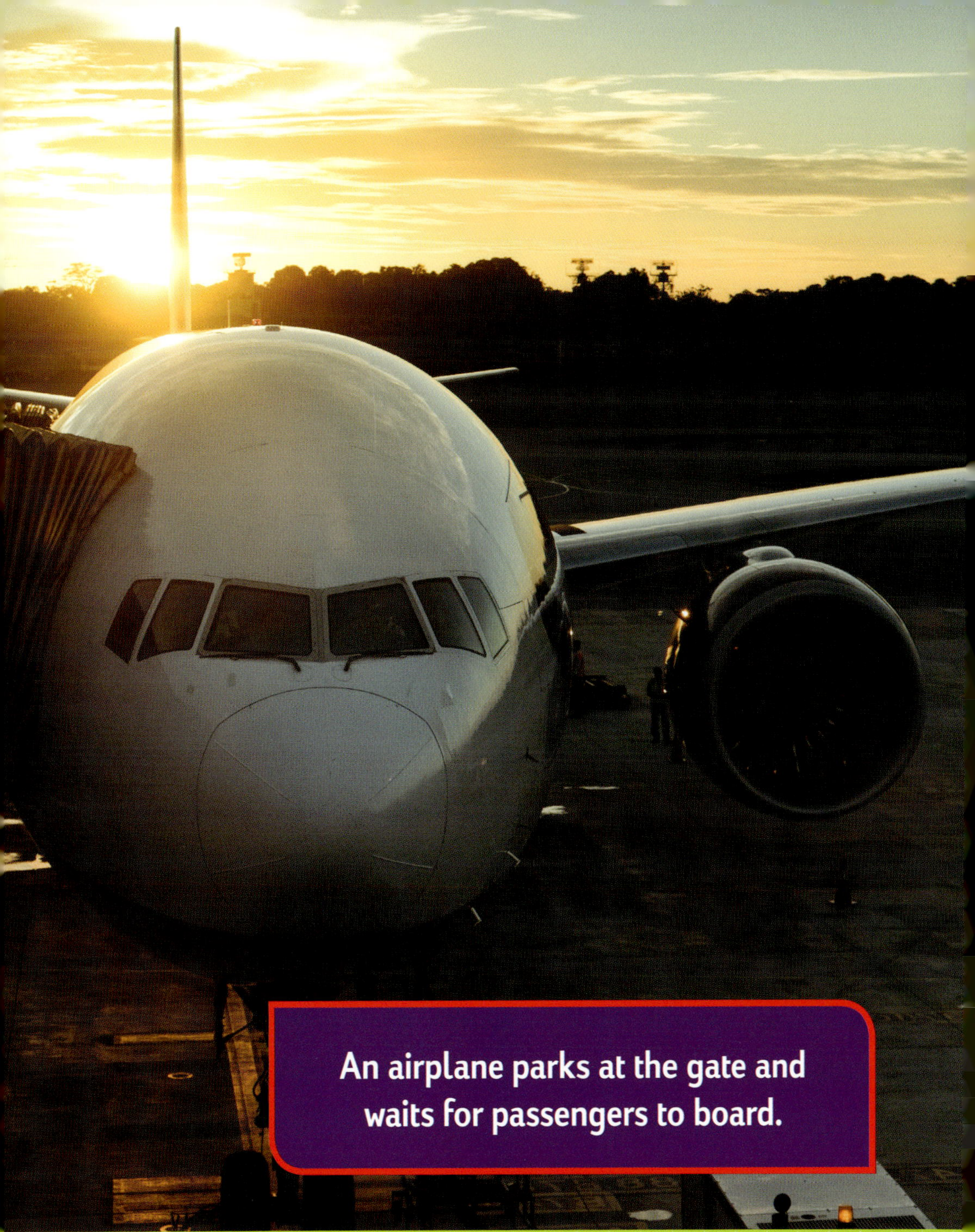

An airplane parks at the gate and waits for passengers to board.

- Architects finish plans for buildings.
- Workers build foundations for the buildings.
- Workers frame and complete the buildings.
- YEAR 7
- The air traffic control tower is built.
- Workers pave the runway and add paint and lights.
- YEAR 8
- **Airplanes take off and land at the new airport.**

GLOSSARY

airport complex A group of airport buildings and structures on the same site; airport complexes include hangars, terminals, parking ramps, public transit stations, and other buildings.

architect Someone who designs buildings and other structures.

blueprint A technical drawing of a building or structure that shows measurements and specifications.

concourse A part of the airport terminal where passengers wait to get on and off airplanes.

contractor A company that hires workers and sets schedules for a building project.

engineer A person who is trained to design and test structures.

frame To build the basic structure of the building with wood or steel beams.

piles A steel beam that is driven into the ground to support a building.

site An area where a structure is built.

terminal A building where passengers get onto and off of airplanes.

READ MORE

Clement, Nathan. *Fly.* Honesdale, Penn.: Boyds Mills Press, 2019.

Gifford, Clive. *How Airports Work.* New York: Lonely Planet Kids, 2018.

Rober, Harold T. *Going on an Airplane.* Minneapolis: Lerner Publications, 2017.

WEBSITES

Behind the Scenes at the Airport: Air Traffic Control
https://www.youtube.com/watch?v=EIKfHOk8rx0

FunKids, Fun Airport Facts!
http://www.funkidslive.com/learn/behind-the-scenes-at-the-airport/fun-airport-facts/#

NASA, How Do Planes Fly?
https://www.nasa.gov/audience/forstudents/k-4/stories/ames-how-do-planes-fly-text.html

INDEX

ABOUT THE AUTHOR

Author and editor Karen Latchana Kenney has written many science books for children and young adults. She loves going to the airport and taking vacations to interesting places. Karen lives in Minneapolis, Minnesota, with her husband and young son.